BUSINESS
LESSONS
WITH
SHARKMASTER, JR.

WHAT A "SMALL" BUSINESS OWNER
LEARNED FROM A BEST SELLING AUTHOR
ABOUT OUTSELLING, OUTMANAGING,
OUTMOTIVATING, AND OUTNEGOTIATING
THE "BIG" COMPETITION

RANDY CLAY

BUSINESS LESSONS WITH SHARKMASTER, JR.

ISBN #0-9725246-0-6
Copyright © 2002 Randall A. Clay
PCI Press
P.O. Box 361
Sand Springs, OK 74063

Library of Congress Cataloging-in-Publishing Data

Clay, Randall 1961

       Business Lessons With Sharkmaster, Jr.
       Randy Clay
       International Standard Book Number 0-9725246-0-6
       1. Success in business I. Title

Printed in the United States of America

10 9 8 7 6 5 4 3 2 1 First U.S. Edition

*"It's safe to stay in the water now -
'Sharkmaster Jr.' can swim
with the best of them!"*

HARVEY B. MACKAY
author of the #1 New York Times bestseller
"Swim with the Sharks Without Being Eaten Alive"

CONTENTS

DEDICATION

When climbing the long ladder of success, it's always good to take a look down and see who is really holding that ladder up. As I look down, there are two people I see that have long been committed to holding the ladder still, regardless of the business challenges we've been through.

Ivan and Jackie, eternity will not be long enough to tell you how much I love you and appreciate the unconditional support you've given me all these years.

You two should know that when guys I know start telling all their "in-law horror stories," I have honestly said, "I'm sorry. I have no idea what you are talking about!"

I love you guys!

Acknowledgments

Obviously, the first guy on my *List of Appreciation* is **Mr. Harvey B. Mackay,** for his indulgence of a small-potatoes business kid from Tulsa. I'm so glad that you wrote that first book back when I needed it most.

Chris Smith, thanks for recommending the book that spring Sunday morning. (As you can see I never forgot that conversation.)

Gretchen Mullen, my first contact with a real live editor. Gretchen you're the "greatest" and still the chief!

And finally, my friend, **Ms. Lorrie Medford C.N.** Thanks for the final inspiration to get off my *Blessed Assurance* and get this book done. You're awesome!

1

CALL IT AN OMEN, A SIGN, OR WHATEVER YOU WANT

It was a Sunday morning in the spring of 1990. Personally, I thought it was going to be just another day that started by taking my young family to church. I remembered that it had been a difficult week at my screen printing business. Not having gone to college, I was beginning to feel the lack of skills that most business people receive from higher education.

In the hall outside the church auditorium, I was visiting with a fellow entrepreneur about some of the management challenges I was having with one of my employees. When I finished describing the situation, he looked at me and told me about a chapter in a book that he had just finished entitled *"It Isn't the People You Fire Who Make Your Life Miserable, It's the People You Don't."* He continued to tell me that the name of the book was *Swim with the Sharks Without Being Eaten Alive*, written by a man named Harvey Mackay. Not being an avid business reader, I smiled and put the recommendation way back on the shelf of my mind.

On the way out, as was my habit, I stopped by my pastor's office to say the usual "great service," but this particular day he hadn't yet made it to his office. I noticed a book on his desk that wasn't a copy of the "good book" I had seen many times before. As I went over to get a closer look at the cover, you can only imagine my puzzled facial expression when I read *Swim with the Sharks Without Being Eaten Alive,* complete with a picture of this Harvey Mackay guy.

You can call it an omen, a sign, or whatever you want, but my lightning-quick mind suggested that I read that book. After lunch, I went down to our local drug store and found a copy that looked just like the one I'd seen on the desk. I remember reading the first half that afternoon and finishing it later that evening. Its overall simplicity overwhelmed me, and it was the first business book that I had ever read that enabled me to apply its philosophies immediately.

The surprising thing was the application of the

principles that Harvey shared actually produced results! I reread that book so many times that every sales negotiation or management situation that presented itself was handled with knowledge that I had embraced by learning the "Mackay Way." It revolutionized the way I thought about business and forever changed the way I conducted myself in the marketplace.

When I started my sign and decal company back in 1983, the only knowledge I had was the skill of how to produce a quality product. I had been married a little over a year and had just turned 22 years old. Most of my time was spent trying to convince potential clients that I could actually produce the signs or decals they were looking for. While most of my contemporaries were finishing up their degrees, I was enrolling in the School of Hard Knocks and didn't even know it.

When I was working the "One-Man Show," things were great. I controlled everything. But as the business grew, I began to realize that I couldn't do this all by myself, and the need for different production equipment was going to be a necessity.

I had no knowledge of finance, accounting, person-nel management, hiring, sales, marketing, or any of the other requirements to build a long lasting business.

For the first 7 years, I struggled because of ignorance. I thought of going back to school, but by 1990 I had a toddler running around the house and a thrilled stay-at-home mom chasing him.

In reality, the biggest revelation I received after reading *Swim with the Sharks* was that even if I had gone back to school, any knowledge I acquired would come, in one form or another, from books. So, for the last ten years I have been a "continually educated student," using every form of business education material available on the planet.

The first thing I learned in my quest for business knowledge was that there were people I could hire (like a lawyer and an accountant) that already possessed the knowledge I would need. These experts would be able to take care of their areas of expertise so that I could concentrate on educating myself toward building my business.

Hopefully, this book will inspire you to realize that the knowledge you need to succeed is probably already recorded within the pages of someone else's experience.

Keep in mind that when you read a business book,

it's not just for entertainment, but for knowledge. And, knowledge is worthless unless it's put to work and produces something beneficial.

I also want to remind you of the age we are currently living in. It's not the agricultural age or the industrial age; it's the *information* age.

You must learn that in this highly competitive business world, most of the successful people you'll meet didn't stop learning after college, and those that possess superior knowledge usually get superior results.

2

Business Lessons Learned About Sales And Negotiations

NOT ALL BUYERS ARE
LIKE FRANKENSTEIN

Over the years, one thing I've learned about selling is that it has always been easier to sell people things they want than it is to sometimes sell them what they need.

When it comes to buyers, they have been trained to keep the purse strings of the company well guarded, and some take on the task like a monster. Cold call sales are the hardest in the world if you don't have the ability to respond correctly to rejection.

The thing that kept me going in the earlier years was that I refused to take rejection personally. I realized they weren't rejecting me, but the need for my product or service. How could they reject me if they didn't know me?

Not long ago I attended a half-day seminar titled, *"Getting, Keeping and Deserving Your Customers."* One of the clichés used in the seminar was, "It's not who you know, but who needs to know you!"

During one of the breaks, I visited with the speaker about what I learned from Harvey to make a bigger impact in my sales career by changing her cliché just a little. It goes like this: *"It's not 'WHO' you know, but 'WHAT' you know about who you know!"*

I've applied this thought to every potential client over the last ten years with great success. I finally realized that as tough as some buyers, clients and customers can be, one thing you can be sure of is that they are HUMAN! And just being human comes with a ton of opportunities to get to hear the likes and dislikes of another person.

As we continued to visit, I told her about my most important lesson on what is now called "relationship selling." Before I could get the setting of the story out, she asked me to share with the group to help her make the point of how to *deserve* a customer.

Back in the early '90s, there was an international drilling company I wanted for a client. I finally got the appointment to visit with the decision maker concerning the first product I wanted to sell. I offered to reproduce samples of their decals at no cost to show an example of our quality and color matching ability.

At our next meeting, I'll never forget what was said: "Randy, your color matching and overall quality surpasses everything we've purchased in the past and even your pricing is below what we have previously paid, but we are going to stay with our current vendor."

I don't know about you, but if there was ever a time to take rejection personally, that would have been the time for me. It seemed like the only chance I had to get in the door and eventually sell them the safety signs they needed on their fleet of oil drilling rigs.

One day, about two years later, I remembered a comment that was made in that rejection meeting. Their company had safety representatives in different parts of the country and each one was responsible for purchasing signs for his or her own division of rigs. I made a phone call to the same buyer that shot down my first proposal, and asked a simple question:

"Do your safety reps buy signs from catalogs?"

"Yes, and they get catalogs from all over the country."

"Would it be possible to get their addresses to send them our sign information?"

"Sure, what's your fax number?"

Now it's one thing to try and sell the tangible, face-to-face, but it's a totally different thing to sell the invisible over the phone. *Just remember that it's more important to start a relationship than it is to close a sale.* If you want to connect, you had better sharpen your conversational skills. Before I call a geographic area, I try to find out what's going on in the prospective buyer's world. I also look for any news that is related to their company. Get creative!

My first call was to Harrold in the Deep South. I introduced myself, letting him know who allowed me to call. I then took a few moments to visit about his career, how long he'd been with the company, and other things that would help me be sensitive to what his business and even personal needs were.

I told him thanks, and that I would send our sign info right out. Knowing that guys in the oil patch love hats, I also mentioned I would send him one of ours.

Little did I know what chain of events that offer would start.

He said he'd give the hat to his son, who had a collection of over five hundred hats. As he listed a few hats his son had collected, he said that the one hat he'd been trying to get for some time was a hat from Neal Adams Oil Well Firefighters in Houston.

When I hung up, I dialed the next number so fast I almost lost a fingernail. I was calling my good friend, Neal Adams.

Being that it only takes about two days to get a package to Alabama from Oklahoma, it shouldn't be hard to figure out what happened when that package reached the Deep South.

I love going to oil industry trade shows and seeing my buddy Harrold dragging another potential sign buyer to my booth. I never realized that those hats would create the best client/salesperson I've ever had.

RANDY'S REMINDER:

WHEN TRYING TO PUT A LIVING SALES RELATIONSHIP TOGETHER, CONNECT TO THE HEART FIRST!

Next In Line

Up until the fall of 2001, "next in line" is where I'd been standing for over 8 years.

One of the most important things I learned from Harvey is that if you are not able to make a sale to a company you really want to do business with, the best place to find yourself on their list of vendors is No. 2.

Here's the truth: If you can get your name on enough lists in the No. 2 slot, sooner or later they will be calling. Now here's how I know this to be true.

Somewhere down the road No.1 is going to mess up, or your prospect will experience something that changes the way it does business. I can't number the times that I've had a call from someone saying something like: "Our senior buyer has just retired, and

I'm kind of new in this position for buying safety signs. I've heard you have a better way of purchasing them than just digging through these catalogs all day." After I lock in the appointment and hang up the phone, the whole place can always hear me yell "YAHOO!"

Back in 2000, a company I had been wanting as a client received a referral that we could print, of all things, trash can decals that remind people to keep their areas clean.

I had already done my homework about the company and knew enough about its production methods to have some suggestions ready that would help streamline the decal applications for its products. After waiting another year and staying in contact with the buyer, it finally happened .

In one of my "just checking to see how you're doing" calls, I found out that the company was changing its logo and was sending the new decal project out for bid. I said I would like to personally set up a time to visit about this new project. (When I hung up, again my team heard another, "YAHOO!")

Knowing that it would be difficult to get the bid because the previous vendor had been locked in for a zillion years, I had to come up with something that would put me on top.

There I sat with the materials manager, product manager, product engineer and a senior buyer. The meeting opened with the usual formal introductions and we began discussing actual production of the new elaborate logo. I explained all the different ways we could do it. The thing I knew that would wake everyone up was when I said, "Would you like to see a production sample next week?"

It was obvious that the engineer didn't seem very excited about being in the meeting, and I knew he would be one that I'd need to have as an ally. In the meeting, he mentioned that he wished someone would develop a small measuring unit that would be easier to affix to the product than the way they've done it for years. You'll never believe what I took to that next meeting in addition to production samples of their new logo. (And then again, if you know me, you would believe it.) In my hand was a prototype of that measuring device that he described the week before. The engineer was so tickled to see it that he played with it the rest of the meeting.

Another couple of weeks went by and just before it came time for the decision to award the contract, I asked if they had a trade show coming up in the near future. They answered, "Yes." I let them know that if they decided to award the contract to my company, I would be glad to mark their display units, new logo and all, absolutely FREE. Now guess who got the contract? Harvey was right! Being in the No. 2 slot is great--if you're ready to start the show when they call your number.

RANDY'S REMINDER:

IF YOU'RE COMMITTED TO WAIT
FOREVER, YOU'LL FIND OUT THAT
IT NEVER TAKES THAT LONG!

Back From The Dead

It was February of 1997. I made just a quick call to one of my major construction clients to see how his stock of job site signs was holding up. I nearly dropped the phone when he said, "Randy, we are going to be using another local company to print our signs because they beat your current price."

If you're like me, I hate hearing those words, especially from a client I *thought* we had a great relationship with for several years. When I inquired about the new price, it was the exact figure I was paying for the unprinted sign blank. I couldn't believe it. As a matter of fact, I never got over it!

As the years went by, I kept hearing information that led me to the conclusion that I lost the relationship due to some questionable ethical practices from one of my vendors. Nevertheless, the toughest thing was driving around town and seeing those signs on their job sites and always wondering if there was anything else I could have done to save the account.

Then one day, in May of 2002, it happened. I was taking my usual monthly tour through my Rolodex file and there was his name. (Here's a point you should never forget: Don't be too quick about removing people from your client list. You never know when the variables may change in your favor.)

I remember saying to myself, "Oh, what could it hurt? Give him a call." I asked him if my competitor was still taking care of his sign needs and the answer was, "yes."

Immediately, without even thinking that I was asking for classified information, I asked, "How much are you paying for those three by sixes I've been seeing around town?" (I figured he'd tell me because he didn't have a problem letting me know the last time price was an issue.) I was surprised and thrilled to hear he was paying $20 more than I was currently charging for the same type of signs.

After going over to his warehouse and hearing a few

really good hunting stories, I picked up the layout he needed on his current signs. He made a comment that will hopefully keep me from losing his valued business again. He said, "Randy, all I'm about is saving money!"

Of course that would have been good information 5 years ago, but there's still nothing that feels as good as a second chance.

RANDY'S REMINDER:
YOUR SALES OPPORTUNITY IS NEVER
REALLY DEAD UNTIL YOU SEE
ITS NAME IN THE PAPER UNDER
"CHAPTER SEVENS."

IT'S ALL ABOUT THEM

The most popular question I'm asked when visiting with a group of salespeople is: "How do you find information about a new or prospective client that you can use to make a long-lasting impression?"

Over the years, I've made it my No. 1 priority to learn as much as I can about the person I desire to do business with. This philosophy comes from Harvey's Lesson No. 3 on salesmanship. He says, *"Knowing something about your customer is just as important as knowing everything about your product."* I have found that one statement to be the most powerful and profitable one I've ever heard.

When it comes to actually finding out information, one of my favorite avenues is to first develop a relationship with the receptionist and/or the personal assistant to the person I'm wanting to reach.

You must realize that the receptionist is the guardian of the fort. He or she can make you or break you when it comes to making contact with the people you need to meet. I want to get to know the receptionist on a first name basis. I usually make small talk before asking to be put through to Mr./Ms. Prospect. I'll ask questions like, "How are things going with you today?" (A word of caution--you need to be prepared for anything, because the receptionist may let you know exactly how things are going.)

Once, after asking that question, my soon-to-be phone buddy let me know that her son was in an auto accident the night before, and even though he was going to be all right, her emotions were at an all time high. Naturally, I spent a few extra minutes encouraging her. Keep this in mind. People can tell if you really care about them, and really caring is the key to developing relationships.

Now, if I get someone that I can tell has a fun personality, I'll say things like, "It's hotter than blazes out today. Do they have the air conditioner vent pointed in your direction? If not, connect me with maintenance and I'll get that taken care of for you." That one usually gets a laugh and an immediate connection to Mr./Ms. P. or at least the assistant.

Personally, I really enjoy working with executive assistants because they've been hired to get things done, and they've proven to me that they can.

Sooner or later, the building of these relationships will develop into a wealth of information that can help me *WOW* a prospect into a client.

RANDY'S REMINDER:
PEOPLE WILL ALWAYS BE DRAWN TO THOSE WHO TAKE A MOMENT TO SHOW TRUE INTEREST!

THE
'IT'S ALL ABOUT THEM'
LUNCH

Another favorite thing I do is what I call the "It's All About Them" lunch. This is where I go to lunch and try not to mention anything about my products or services, instead letting the prospect tell me about him or herself.

I usually start by asking something like, "Tell me, are you originally from (whatever city we are having lunch in)?" That is usually all it takes to get someone going.

One recent lunch I had was with a safety director from a large company here in Tulsa. He told me he was from Kansas and was transferred when the company he was working for was purchased by one here in Oklahoma.

He was really enjoying telling me about his high school football days and his favorite pro team. But the thing he was the most excited about was his ten year wedding anniversary the next week. He mentioned a great bed and breakfast he found just outside Oklahoma City, and that he and his wife were very excited to be able to get away for a few days. He told me that they were about to finish building their new house, and that his wife and children had been staying with her parents in another city. I could definitely understand his anticipation about their time together.

Surely by now you can see an opportunity to make an impression and, believe me, I took it.

When I got back to the office I found the bed and breakfast on the Internet and gave it a call. I asked if there was someone locally that could make a fantastic gift basket for a couple celebrating an anniversary there next week. Of course, there was a company that could take care of me.

The week after the anniversary trip, I received *the phone call*. I loved the excitement in his voice as he told me that at first they thought this humongous basket of everything you could imagine was courtesy of the bed and breakfast--until his wife later read the card. He couldn't believe it!

Needless to say, I have done tens of thousands of dollars with his company, and my initial investment was only a lunch and a $45 gift basket.

RANDY'S REMINDER:

CONTINUED BUSINESS USUALLY FOLLOWS THOSE WHO INVEST IN SOMEONE ELSE'S BUSINESS.

3

BUSINESS LESSONS LEARNED ABOUT CUSTOMER SERVICE

'CAN I GET SOME HELP OVER HERE?'

We've all experienced it. Waiters and waitresses that act as if you're invisible. Going to a department store and figuring out that it would be easier to find the "lost ark" than it is to find a sales clerk. Or how about calling your favorite electronics store to listen to the melodious sound of eternal ringing? I have found that when some companies want to connect you with customer service, what they have overlooked is the one thing that determines whether or not they even have a customer service department.

True customer service has always depended on having a "customer servant" that can be reached without exerting a tremendous amount of effort and time.

Everyone has seen the American stereotype servant in the movies: nannies, butlers, maids and chauffeurs. Even though it's Hollywood, the characters exhibit a sense of pride in who they work for and quickly see to it that their employers' needs are met. Can you imagine what your business could do if your employees or co-workers realized that customers were actually *paying* to have their needs taken care of?

Over the nearly twenty years of being in business I have tried to develop the "customer servant mentality." I have learned to know my customers' needs as individuals, and not as a list of products they are interested in.

"Customer servanthood" is all about being willing and ready to serve the very moment the phone rings or the customer walks through the front door.

After I graduated from high school, I had an opportunity to work at a local department store. I quickly became the manager of the art and school supplies department. As the summer was coming to a close, I had an idea about how to better serve the mothers that would be coming in to buy school supplies for the next school year. I went to all the local schools and asked for each grade level's list of supplies.

I placed an order to adequately take care of the needs of those that would be shopping down my aisles. Since the lists were almost identical, I stocked the shelves in the order they appeared on the lists.

The enjoyable thing was when mothers came in and looked a little hurried or overwhelmed. I just calmly took the basket and filled the order for them.

The store manager let me know numerous times how those mothers couldn't believe how well I'd taken care of them.

Here are a few questions to help you get a pulse on your customer service activities.

1. Do you care, not only if, but HOW your customer receives what is needed from you or your company?

2. Do you have the answers to questions that might be asked about your service or products? Can you give intelligent recommendations?

3. Do you use voice mail more than necessary to inadvertently delay service to your customer?

4. Are you known for returning messages in minutes, hours, or days?

5. Do you fuel the fire of unsatisfied customers by your attitude, or do you help them focus on the issue of serving them to right any wrong?

6. When a problem arises regarding an order that appears to be out of your control, do you call the customer and give the status, or an explanation and a possible concession?

7. If you absolutely cannot get what the customer needs, do you have a network that can?

If you answered "no" to the first question, the rest of them won't even matter. It really boils down to an attitude of caring.

Determine not to be like those companies that can't seem to get their customer service issues solved. Sometimes, it's evident that their copy of the golden rule has a different plating on it. It has the look and heaviness of lead.

RANDY'S REMINDER:

YOU'LL ALWAYS FIND CUSTOMERS THAT
WILL NEVER MIND PAYING FOR SERVICE
THAT'S PREMIUM AND UNLEADED.

DEFUSING THE DISGUSTED!

Correct me if I'm wrong, but I have found only one business where the customer doesn't care one iota what kind of service he or she is receiving. And, since most of us aren't in the funeral business, there will come a day, sooner or later, when you will encounter a living, breathing (often heavily breathing), unhappy customer.

Recently I received a phone call letting me know that on an Internet bulletin board someone had posted a comment that they were "very unhappy" about a product they had purchased from me. We've all heard the stats on how many people can find out about your shortcomings when someone didn't get what they expected. The Internet has now taken that to an unbelievable level.

First, I tried to e-mail the dissatisfied party and guess what? The e-mail address wasn't working. After spending a few days trying to figure out who it was so that I could get him or her back into "happyland," I finally realized I had to post my own note in hopes of calming the rest of the potential customers within the association.

I knew from the bulletin that there wasn't going to be an opportunity to fix the oversight, so my plan was simple. In most cases, nothing calms the irritated customer quicker than a full, no strings attached R-E-F-U-N-D!

In my response, I asked the mystery customer if he had tried to contact us about the problem, emphasizing that the most important thing to us now was to totally refund any investment, including freight, if we just knew where to send it. I even thanked the customer for allowing us the opportunity to provide the product in the first place. I also put a side note to anyone else that had problems to call my 1-800 number and we would fix it immediately.

A couple of days later, I received another phone call that said, "Have you seen the bulletin board? ... It's turned into a Randy Clay Company Lovefest!"

Sure enough, a couple of extremely satisfied customers had posted comments about how well we'd taken care of them and that we were the best supplier they'd ever dealt with. Finally, the "Cheers" beat the "Jeers" 2-to-1.

By the way, I thought you'd like to know--the "Unhappy Publisher" never did call for that refund. I guess he was just having a bad day.

RANDY'S REMINDER:
IF YOU THINK A REFUND IS COSTLY WAIT UNTIL YOU SEE THE PRICE OF "LOST BUSINESS"

4

BUSINESS LESSONS LEARNED ABOUT MANAGEMENT AND WORK ETHIC

Fixing The Boat While It's Still Afloat

There is nothing quite like the feeling you get as you are sitting comfortably at your desk, when you notice a manager or employee standing in your doorway, white as a ghost who says ... "We have a little problem."

In the early years of my business career, my first thought after hearing those words was, *we* can't include *me*, because I was just sitting here minding my own business.

But as the years pass by, the realization becomes very clear that if you are at the helm of your ship, you'd better be ready when you get the report that someone just knocked a hole in the bottom of your boat. It shouldn't be too hard to figure out that if the boat you are responsible for is going down, you had better be proficient at taking quick and positive action, unless of course, you've somehow learned to walk on water.

I'll never forget one particular day that was very much like the one I've just described. When I got the report of a *problem,* it was the only thing my production manager could get out of his mouth. It seemed like it took only an atomic second before my brain figured out what the only possible problem at the beginning of this major contract could be. In less than thirty minutes, the team had mistakenly produced over eight hundred petroleum pipeline markers with a material cost near $2,000. I'm talking about a material that couldn't be recycled or cleaned off--it was a total loss.

When my manager told me that the first person responsible was about to start crying, my first thought was, "Tell him to hold up a second and I'll come back there to join him!" I was, however, surprised by such an emotional response, because in the near twenty years I've operated this company, I have never raised my voice, verbally abused, or belittled an employee for a mistake. I've also experienced, the majority of the time, that my team members are usually harder on themselves than I would ever be.

As you can imagine, team paralysis was starting to set in and productivity was swirling down the drain. It was time to take action if we wanted to stay afloat.

I would like to submit the following for consideration the next time you have to correct a mistake with the goal of maintaining the overall morale.

1. Check your eyes for railroad ties.

When a team member makes a mistake, it's usually because he or she overlooked something. Before you begin checking or trying to clear up someone else's eyesight, make sure that you have a clear picture yourself and be absolutely sure you didn't contribute to the inaccuracy. Things like incomplete information or ordering incorrect materials or supplies won't put you high on the Great Manager's Ballot.

2. If you plan to use that pile of rocks on your desk, make sure your nameplate reads ... GOD!

In ancient times, stoning someone to death in public was the ultimate fix for mistakes. Today, some managers get a high from throwing insults, hurling profanities, and trying to belittle the "mistake maker" in front of peers. Every one of us has probably been in that situation and can still remember the embarrassment and humiliation that came with it.

If you have to correct someone, do it privately and remember, team members will always produce better if they aren't concerned about "dodging rocks."

3. *Know the difference between an* incident *and a* problem.

This is an easy one. You'll find that an incident is usually something that has never happened this way before. Make sure everyone involved understands why it happened, and always have a plan to keep it from happening again. If you see an incident happen again and again, you now have a problem.

4. *Don't build memorials with the products of failure.*

Going back to the day I started this lesson with, I knew that morale was the most valuable thing I couldn't afford to lose *and* stay on schedule. The material that was produced incorrectly stood close to three feet high. I told my manager to remove the "monument" from the production area immediately.

I'll never forget hearing those stacks of plastic hitting the bottom of the dumpster. I remember thinking, "BOOM" ... $500, "BOOM" … $1000, "BOOM" … $1500, and finally "KABOOM"... $2000.

After I wiped my brow, I realized I didn't want any reminder staring the team in the face as they were trying to recover and make the due date.

I think Harvey summed it up the best when he said, *"It doesn't matter how many pails of milk you lose, as long as you don't lose the cow!"*

RANDY'S REMINDER:

HOLES IN YOUR BOAT NOT REPAIRED CORRECTLY ONLY GET BIGGER!

Clichés That Kill ...

The person that came up with the old phrase, "Sticks and stones may break my bones, but words will never hurt me" was either hard-of-hearing or completely deaf.

The fact of the matter is that words are the most powerful things we possess in the shaping of our personal worlds and also the worlds of others.

I know that you've seen people that soared and excelled when given a positive affirmation and also people that felt belittled and even worthless at a nonconstructive critical comment. It's amazing to me that some of the things that we say have little or no thought behind them because we've heard them so often we repeat them like a parrot. One thing about words we need to always remember is that they are supposed to paint pictures. For instance when I say "cat" do you think C-A-T ... or do you picture an actual cat? When I have the opportunity to share with people about this subject, I always emphasize the importance of speaking words that paint pictures of success instead of pictures of failure.

There are a few clichés I have learned to eliminate from my vocabulary over the years, like "What you don't know can't hurt you." I found out the opposite is more true, and some things you don't know can actually kill you! I've learned that there are certain things in business that if you don't know them, can destroy the business or continually stunt its growth.

The unfortunate thing that many don't realize is that the things we allow to come out of our mouths really do determine the level of success we see in our business and personal lives.

The good ol' boy that uses his mouth to continually criticize his boss and/or fellow employees, wife or "old lady," and his "never-gonna-amount-to-anything" kids, shouldn't be too disappointed when he becomes jobless, lonely and the father of a dysfunctional next generation.

The next cliché that really gets me is when I used to hear my UPS buddy leave and say, "Don't work too hard!" The reason that I know that phrase is just a non-thinking cliché is because I don't know one UPS delivery person that doesn't have the appearance of working hard. Years ago I came up with my own cliché as an answer to that one. I simply say, "Thanks. I wish I could take that recommendation, but not today!" Please don't misunderstand. I do try to implement "the work smarter, not harder" process, but experience has shown me that both really work great together. However, I have seen some people take the "don't work too hard" thought too seriously.

The last cliché I want you to think about is one I can't stand! I have always been an employer that wants to know what ideas and thoughts someone on the team can bring to the planning table. My team learned years ago that the answer to my question, "What do you think?" should never be, "I try not to." For some people, it's obvious that this response may be true if you look at the mistakes they continue to make.

The expanded version of the above killer cliché is, "They don't pay me to think!" Now I would understand this coming from someone who always had his or her ideas put on the back burner, but the people that are fluent in this kind of communication often have the just-get-by mentality.

One day I was inspired to make a safety sign that has become quite popular. It reads: *"BEFORE STARTING WORK PLEASE ENGAGE YOUR BRAIN!"*

I want to challenge you to take an inventory of your vocabulary and speaking habits. Ask yourself if the things you are constantly saying are actually adding to your life or taking away from it.

If your work situation isn't what you'd like it to be, see if there is any adjustment you could make in the things you say about or to your employer or fellow employees. Do the same in your other relationships as well. I'll bet when you change the way you talk, you'll see a change in your quality of life.

RANDY'S REMINDER:

I HAVE HEARD ALL MY LIFE THAT IT'S BETTER TO KEEP YOUR MOUTH CLOSED AND LET PEOPLE THINK YOU'RE A FOOL THAN TO OPEN IT AND REMOVE ALL DOUBT.

No Reward For The Outlaw Employee

In the beginning of the 20th century, history tells us about a cub reporter that was given the mission of a lifetime. Andrew Carnegie, the early century steel giant, commissioned this young writer to devote twenty years of his life to researching and inter- viewing the most prestigious, respected and wealthiest men in the world of industry.

The goal of this writer was to document the philosophy behind these men's successes. One of the keys that these businessmen saw as mandatory to achieve financial success is surprisingly overlooked today. This key is also referred to as an actual law and I'm thankful that I learned to apply it when I entered the working world.

It has definitely been one of the reasons that I have made it this far in my business career.

It's called the "Law of Increasing Returns."

One of the things over the years I have come to detest is the attitude that basically says, "I'm not going to do anything more than I have to do in order to get a paycheck."

After a while I found that the paycheck all of a sudden isn't big enough anymore, and some people begin to think that they should make more money just because they've been around a long time. With all the layoffs and downsizing we have seen, I hope people are starting to see that just because you show up doesn't necessarily mean you're worth keeping.

Several months ago I had the opportunity to share with a group about work ethic and a subject that some people hate, called "Doing More Than Paid For." A few weeks later a young man that was in the audience came up to me and told me that my stories inspired him to change his attitude toward work and the way he approached each day.

He began to arrive at the machine shop thirty minutes early every day and started working before everyone else showed up. He did it with an attitude that it didn't matter whether he was ever paid for it or not. Two weeks later, his employer gave him a surprise raise.

The next time I saw him I asked him if he was still doing what he had started and, to my disappointment, he said "no." When I asked why, he said he buckled under the persecution and name calling of the other employees. They were making references to the color of his nose and telling him that he was making them look bad. I almost went nuts.

"That is exactly what I said would happen when I was challenging you to go the extra mile," I reminded him. I asked him who he was there to please? Hadn't his employer responded appropriately by giving him a raise?

The next time someone tells you that you are making them look bad, it should be obvious that they don't need any assistance from you. I'll bet they are doing a great job on their own!

Employees that have the "just do enough to get by" attitude will one day wonder why they aren't getting by! The oldest version of the "Law of Increasing

Returns" is the "Law of Seedtime and Harvest." Think about it ... have you ever just planted one seed and only gotten one seed back? Of course not, because we'd all starve to death! The same is true in the workplace--if you give a little more than is expected, then sooner or later it's going to come back in the form of something you need.

If you understand the law we've been talking about, you should realize the only thing that gives you the right to ask for more money, benefits, etc., is the fact that you have earned them in advance. You wouldn't ever be upset with your garden if it didn't produce something you didn't plant in advance, would you? Yet people don't seem to get it.

Here's a thought ... when it comes to a possible layoff, who should they let go first? An *asset* or the *liability*?

RANDY'S REMINDER:

IF YOU'RE NOT RENDERING MORE SERVICE THAN YOU'RE BEING PAID FOR, THEN YOU MAY BE STUCK ONLY BEING PAID FOR WHAT YOU ARE RENDERING.

5

Business Lessons Learned About Networking (With People)

YOUR PERSONAL
WHEEL OF FORTUNE

There is a phrase connected with prime time television that has paralleled the subject of high finance. When a person has spoken these four simple words followed by its corresponding action, one of three things will usually happen. They will stay where they are financially, increase financially, or lose everything that they have recently accumulated. The phrase is, *"I Think I'll Spin."* Untold millions of dollars have been won and lost by the action following this little phrase.

For decades, television viewers have shown their enthusiasm for America's number one prime time game show, ***Wheel of Fortune.***

Years ago, I found a wheel that is just as much fun

and profitable as Pat and Vanna's "Mega Spinner." Not only has it become a valuable part of my financial and social life, it has continued to grow every day for the last ten years. Believe it or not, I'm about to tell you about my *Rolodex*.

One of the most valuable things I've been able to observe and apply to my life is learning how successful people are fanatics about meeting, staying in touch, and really developing human-to-human relationships. With all of the communication technology available today, I personally don't think anything can compare to the voice of someone you want to visit with.

Every morning, my Rolodex sits ready to make a difference in my day, and possibly in the day of someone I've taken an interest in. If I could only recall all the times I've been at my desk and said, *"I think I'll spin,"* and without fail, I always find a few names in that fan of cards that I know could use a call from me. Whether it's a checkup on the latest family adventure, a quick reminder of who just turned a year older, or the traditional business call that turns into an actual addition to the monthly sales report, it's always a profitable visit. When calling a client, I never get tired of hearing him or her say, "I've been meaning to call you," or "Oh, my gosh! I was supposed to call you two weeks ago!"

When thinking about a Rolodex, some people might say, "Come on Randy, step into the 21st century. A Rolodex is a relic of history and the way of the future is the electronic database." Now, don't misunderstand, I'm as lap-topped and palm-piloted as the next guy, but the point I'm wanting to make is that it's not about the type of system you use, but how you take care of what the system represents.

In my Rolodex, there are abundant opportunities to enhance my life in the area of financial and business wisdom. It also contains a host of influences that promote a positive attitude about life in general. I get all of this with a simple spin and the realization that people are the only true fortune that I have.

I realize that a tremendous amount of today's commerce is done electronically by purchase orders, bank transfers, and now, online shopping. However, we need to always remember that behind every transaction, there is a "someone" that needs our product, service, or sometimes just an encouraging word.

Recently, I was asked what was something I wish I had known when I started my company back in 1983. My answer was one that I learned from Harvey: "Most entrepreneurs need to realize the most important word in the English language for business people isn't even in the dictionary. It's spelled *R-O-L-O-D-E-X.* "

RANDY'S REMINDER:

A TRUE WHEEL OF FORTUNE
WILL NEVER HAVE ROOM FOR
A SPACE MARKED BANKRUPT!

LETHARGIC NETWORKS

We all need to realize that a network of contacts is only as good as the benefits it provides. Real success is highly dependent upon the relationships you've developed. There is never a day that goes by that I haven't tried to meet someone new, get to know something about that person and immediately add the name to my Rolodex.

One of my most recent additions occurred during an afternoon of golf. My golf coach Paul and I had our tee time and were told we'd be paired up with another duo. Apparently the other two were running a little behind and just as I was about to attempt a swing, here they came.

After the introductions, I asked them to kindly look

the other way to hopefully keep myself from being totally embarrassed. They said, "Oh that's all right, we haven't played in months." I immediately thought, 'yeah right'-- it's probably because you're taking a break from the PGA tour.

In the usual "what do you do" conversations, I learned that they were brothers and the owners of two very prominent restaurants in Tulsa.

Talk about two great guys--they spared no enthusiasm when I shot my first birdie ever. We were marching around the green giving high fives and the whole bit. What a day. The icing on the cake was when we exchanged business cards and a week later I received a gift certificate to one of their restaurants.

The point of this little lesson is to remind you that everyone you meet is important and worth putting in your network. That same afternoon I had my assistant enter them in my Rolodex. I called a few days later to thank him for the gift and told him to give me a call the next time they play.

However, a contact file is profitless unless it is used. I don't know about you, but maintaining my network is as important to me as my vehicle maintenance because I'm extremely dependent on both to get me somewhere in life.

RANDY'S REMINDER:
IF YOU'RE GOING TO BE LAZY IN AN AREA, NEVER LET IT BE IN YOUR RELATIONSHIPS.

START THE CONVERSATION

You wouldn't believe how many calls I've received recently from friends that have been forced to make a career change. The ones I'm really excited about are those who have decided to give the art of selling a shot.

As I mentioned at the beginning of this book, we are living in the "Information Age," and a lot of companies are betting on the Internet to someday replace the living, breathing, flesh-and-blood salesperson. The funny thing is that most of us that are dabbling on the 'Net still haven't figured out how to stay on the first page of the search engine list.

One of the greatest thrills I get is sharing with the beginner salesperson a few things that will put him or her ahead of the competition.

Several months ago, I had the opportunity to moderate a discussion at one of our Tulsa Chamber of Commerce Network Breakfasts. I had submitted 3 questions that each table would discuss among themselves. The third question I came up with was based upon the need to help the freshman salesperson overcome the pull of the *comfort zone*. The question was, *"How do you get from the comfort zone to the end zone?"* With that question, I submitted a story about mastering the ability of talking to anybody at anytime.

Finishing a semi-weekly shopping tour through my favorite home improvement store, I finally wound up at the checkout counter. In front of me was a man purchasing a bucket load of $50 gift cards. I couldn't help it. I tapped him on the shoulder and said, *"Excuse me, but could you tell me what it would take to be allowed into the circle of your closest friends?"*

When he looked at me, I was staring at the pile of cards on the counter. He busted up laughing and said one of the guys at his office suggested these cards as a give-away for a golf tournament his company was hosting.

While we were waiting for his credit card company to be convinced that someone hadn't stolen his card for such a large purchase ($2500, if my memory serves me right), I found out he was the VP of a company I had been wanting to do business with.

After exchanging information, he told me to give him a call and he'd connect me with his purchasing person.

I'm still doing business with his company, and you should be convinced that if you've got something to sell, you'll never know if someone wants to buy unless you start asking.

RANDY'S REMINDER:

TOUCHDOWNS ARE NEVER MADE BY
THOSE WHO ARE TOO SCARED
TO GET OFF THE BENCH.

6

BUSINESS LESSONS LEARNED ABOUT APPRECIATION

SOONER OR LATER, CREDIT IS DUE!

Not too long ago, I was taking the scheduled inventory of my life and when I came to the area of entertainment I asked myself, "Why are you such a fanatic about *NASCAR* racing?" As I began to evaluate all the possible reasons, I knew that it wasn't necessarily the fun of watching cars go around in circles for most of an afternoon at speeds that get close to 200 mph. After several minutes, I figured it out.

As far back as I can remember, the only thing that I ever wanted to be was a professional artist. Through my formative years it became more refined, and I desired to become a commercial artist. I can still remember dreaming about one day making a living by creating corporate logos. When I was in my junior year of high school, my commercial art class was sandwiched in between 2 screen printing classes. I was so convinced that this was the skill I wanted to learn that I opted to go to work for a screen printing firm after a shot at college didn't work out.

Jim Cypert, owner of Ad-Cal Company in Tulsa, allowed me the beginning of what is now my career. It wasn't in the creation of company identities where I found satisfaction, but in producing the finished product.

You name it, I printed everything from equipment decals to corporate parking stickers. As I reflect on the joy that I have today producing corporate images in one form or another, I finally realized that *NASCAR* and I have a couple of things in common.

The first obvious thing is the need to be surrounded by corporate logos.

The second, however, is what happens at the end of the race in victory lane. When a driver emerges from his car, he usually jumps up on top of the roof and showers his team and admirers with *Pepsi*, *Coke* or *Gatorade*. When he jumps down from his victor's pedestal, he begins an interview with a commentator from the hosting network. After a few details concerning the race, he begins a tidal wave of appreciation for the sponsors on his car.

Allow me to pose a question. "When was the last time you showed appreciation for those who sponsored you as you have competed in the wild world of business?" Regardless of the fact that you may not be where you want to be with your definition of success, you probably are not where you were, say, 5 or ten years ago. Let me give you a simple plan to help you give a little credit where credit is due.

You will need to make *3 lists* that will contain the names of those people that have helped and influenced you to become the success that you are today.

The *first list* should contain family and friends that have really made a positive impact in your life.

The *second list* is for former teachers, managers, employers or suppliers.

The *third list* is for customers or clients that maybe aren't receiving the appreciation they should be getting already.

After you have made your lists, start adding addresses and phone numbers to each name. If you are the type that expresses yourself better by writing, then make sure you get a stack of thank you cards.

It is important to have your phone lists and or cards ready to go. Then make a 4 week plan to start sending your cards, or making phone calls during breaks, a few minutes at lunch, and maybe a few minutes in the evening. Attempt to have each list completed a week at a time. During the fourth week, you may want to have lunch or dinner with a few of your "Hall of Fame" inductees.

I can promise you that at the end of this process, not only will you be feeling great, but you will probably hear the words ... "You made my day!"

RANDY'S REMINDER:

IT'S GOOD EVERY NOW AND THEN TO
GET OUT OF THE "RACE CAR OF LIFE"
AND GIVE A CHEER FOR THOSE WHO
HAVE SPONSORED YOU ON YOUR
TRACK OF SUCCESS!

FINALLY MEETING
HARVEY

I've had a number of people comment that they loved my story about finally meeting my long distance and literary mentor, Harvey Mackay.

As impossible as it seemed that I would ever meet him, I'm reminded that it doesn't matter how impossible your dreams seem to be, if you hang on to them long enough, you'll see the majority come true.

Every year starting in 1990, I called Harvey's assistant Greg Bailey to ask if Harvey was going to be anywhere near Tulsa for a speaking engagement, and the answer was always "not this year."

In January of 2000 you can imagine the shock when Greg said, "Randy, you're not going to believe it." Sure enough, he was coming to Tulsa on February 17 to speak. All I wanted to know was, "Who do I call?"

I finally made contact with the woman in charge of the reservations, and she informed me that she only had a few tickets left and she'd be glad to send me one.

Even though hearing him speak was next on my wish list, I honestly didn't think I'd have a chance to actually meet him.

I arrived early to find my seat and then I went on the hunt to find that nice woman that made this day possible. After finding her and giving my sincerest thanks, she asked the question that I had been waiting to hear for what seemed to be forever: "Would you like to meet him?"

My only regret was that I didn't bring a book for him to sign, but fortunately he was giving everyone a copy of his book *Rolodex Network Builder,* which I put in my pocket when I found my seat.

I'll never forget his first words after we were introduced: "You wrote me a letter, didn't you?"

With a puzzled look I answered, "Yes sir, I did." He then pointed at my lapel. I was wearing the shark pin he sent me when he wrote me back.

"I only sent those pins to the people that personally

wrote me," he said, "and as a matter of fact, I personally answered over 300,000 letters." (I still wonder if I heard him right, but knowing him and how he operates I would never doubt it.)

He then asked, "Do you have all my books?"

I replied, "Yes sir, all in hardback."

"How about my tape series?"

"Yes sir."

"Even my latest one?"

"Are you talking about the one with the two bonus tapes? That was an excellent series," I said with a smile.

I then commented that the one thing I didn't have was his autograph in one of his books. I pulled the Rolodex book out of my coat pocket, which he gladly signed. "You don't have a copy of this book, do you?" he asked.

"As a matter of fact, I have 2 other ones," I answered proudly. I'll never forget his smile.

One of Harvey's famous sayings is: "Never say 'no' for the other guy." In other words, make a presentation and if you get rejected, *big deal,* because you'll never know the answer until you ask.

I had heard that the format of this particular meeting was one where they encouraged you to write a question on a 3-by-5 index card and they would randomly select a few for him to answer. Knowing the chances of him picking my card were leaning toward the impossible side, I prepared a 2 sided full-color card with a special request.

As we were finishing, I pulled the card out of my pocket. It had a shark bite out of the corner and it asked him to consider co-authoring a book with me in 2008 (the 20th anniversary of *Swim with the Sharks*).

He chuckled and said, "Randy I won't promise that I'll write a book with you, but I can probably help you get yours published."

As we were walking out, he turned to me and said, "I know one thing you don't have. Call my secretary and tell her to send you one of my 'Shark Ties' and get yourself a blue suit to wear with it."

And that is exactly what I did!

RANDY'S REMINDER:

WHEN YOU FINALLY MEET THE PERSON
THAT HAS MADE A DIFFERENCE IN
YOUR LIFE, DON'T FORGET THE
TWO MOST IMPORTANT WORDS...
THANK YOU!

7

THE ECONOMY OF
YOU

In closing, I'm kind of curious to know what and how you're thinking right now about the economy.

Not about the national economy, but about your personal and/or business economy.

Since September 11th of 2001, we continue to see more tragedies in other areas besides the ones we graphically viewed in New York, Washington D.C. and Pennsylvania.

The layoffs and the corporate disasters we've seen are almost beyond comprehension. It seems like every cover of your favorite business magazine has a main story about a *big company* on the brink of destruction.

I want to remind you that no matter where you find yourself in this time of uncertainty, *you* are still the greatest asset you possess. The question is, when things begin to slow down or completely fall out from under you, what do you do in response? If you take too long to recover, you could miss the next opportunity that is just around the corner.

Recently I was visiting with a friend that was a manager for a well known telecommunications company. Over the years, he has asked my opinion about different business ideas and I have always thought he had above average entrepreneurial tendencies. On this recent visit he said, "I guess I'm going to be an entrepreneur now." When I asked him why now, he said, "I was laid off last week."

It's amazing to see the response that people have when their imagined security is taken away. I commented that it sounds like he is no longer just "interested" in seeing what he can accomplish, but is now "committed" to doing something different.

It's also amazing to see how creative we can get when we have to be. The sad part is, once we begin to really tap into the potential of doing something big, the only regret we usually have is that we didn't do it sooner. I guess I'll never understand why people have such a hard time doing the one thing that separates us from all creation. The ability to *think!*

I realize that Corporate America has been successful by the continual creation of systems that have taken away the need for thinking, and the result has been more streamlined production and a reduction in mistakes. But what happens to the human part of the system when they are no longer needed and get caught in the ejection seat?

Those that know me have found out that I'm always on a self-improvement adventure and constantly looking for those who want to go with me. If we quit working on ourselves, we are destined to become victims of this world's economy when it takes a nose dive like we've been seeing.

I personally enjoy getting a call or e-mail from a friend or business associate to bounce an idea off all this knowledge I've been hoarding up. I'm thoroughly convinced that most of the problems we face have already been solved and the answers are located in the millions of books and self-help tapes that have been published. All the knowledge you need to change your life is waiting on you!

If you have recently found yourself back in the job market or considering a career change, I want to encourage you to start tuning yourself up today. It would be a pity if the greatest opportunity ever to unveil itself would be missed because you were looking down in discouragement.

Yes, there is turmoil in the world today, but there are people looking to you to see how you are going to respond. Get the "dis" out of your courage and get moving!

RANDY'S REMINDER:

WORK HARDER ON YOURSELF
THAN YOU DO ON YOUR CAREER,
SO IF THE LATTER FALLS OUT FROM
UNDER YOU, YOU'LL LAND ON YOUR FEET!

ABOUT THE AUTHOR

Randy Clay was born and raised in Tulsa, OK.

His lifelong dream of becoming a commercial artist was realized in 1983 when he started his own commercial screen printing company with an emphasis on corporate identification and logo production.

Randy's company now manufactures all types of safety signs and decals for the oil and gas industries.

His writing and public speaking include various subjects that communicate positive attitude and reaching your personal potential. His desire, wherever he goes, is to help people realize they are born with a mission to accomplish something great.

Randy and his wife Melanie are raising two future business investors, Joshua and Caleb, and live in Sand Springs, a suburb of Tulsa.

Randy can be reached through his website: *www.sharkmasterjr.com.*

Notes Of Inspiration

_____

_____

_____

_____

_____

_____

_____

_____

_____

_____

_____

_____

_____

_____

_____

_____

_____

NOTES OF INSPIRATION

NOTES OF INSPIRATION

_____

_____

_____

_____

_____

_____

_____

_____

_____

_____

_____

_____

_____

_____

_____

_____

_____

NEED ADDITIONAL COPIES?

FOR CREDIT CARD ORDERS
CALL 1-800-678-2529

TO ORDER ONLINE
VISIT OUR WEBSITE AT
WWW.SHARKMASTERJR.COM

FOR MAIL ORDERS
SEND CHECK OR MONEY ORDER
FOR $9.95 PLUS $2.00 S/H
FOR EACH BOOK TO
PCI PRESS
PO BOX 361
SAND SPRINGS, OK 74063

FOR QUANTITY DISCOUNT
INFORMATION CALL
1-800-678-2529
OR E-MAIL
SALES@SHARKMASTERJR.COM